ZADAR T...

2024

"Your Companion to witnessing the best of ZADAR, day trip holiday, beaches, hiking, adventure, valentine's delight, culture and festival, top tourist attractions and hidden gems"

ANGELA DARLINGTON

TABLE OF CONTENTS

3

Introduction

Welcome to the "ZADAR Travel Guide 2024," your ultimate companion to exploring the enchanting city of Zadar in Croatia. This guide has been meticulously crafted to provide comprehensive information, insider tips, and practical advice to make your trip to Zadar a memorable experience. Whether you are a first-time visitor or a seasoned traveler, this guide is designed to cater to your needs and enhance your journey in Zadar.

About This Guide

The "ZADAR Travel Guide 2024" results from extensive research, local insights, and updated information to offer you the most relevant and accurate details about Zadar. It covers various topics, including attractions, accommodations, dining, transportation, practical tips, and more. Each section is designed to give you a deep understanding of Zadar's rich history, vibrant culture, and stunning landscapes, ensuring you make the most of your time in this captivating city.

Why Visit Zadar?

Zadar, situated on Croatia's stunning Dalmatian Coast, is a hidden gem waiting to be discovered by travelers seeking authentic experiences and breathtaking beauty. Here are compelling reasons why Zadar should be at the top of your travel list:

1. Historical Significance: Zadar boasts a rich historical heritage dating back to Roman times, evident in its well-preserved ancient monuments, churches, and archaeological sites such as the Roman Forum and St. Donatus Church.

2. Natural Wonders: From its picturesque coastline and crystal-clear waters to stunning

sunsets admired from the famous Sea Organ waterfront installation, Zadar offers unparalleled natural beauty that mesmerizes visitors.

3. Cultural Fusion: As a meeting point of diverse cultures, including Roman, Venetian, and Croatian influences, Zadar presents a unique blend of architecture, cuisine, and traditions that reflect its multifaceted history.

4. Art and Innovation: Zadar is renowned for its modern art installations, such as the Sea Organ and Greeting to the Sun, which creatively integrate nature, technology, and art to offer visitors immersive experiences.

5. Gateway to Dalmatia: With its strategic location, Zadar is an ideal base for exploring the stunning Dalmatian Coast, nearby islands like Pag and Ugljan, and national parks such as Paklenica and Krka.

How to Use This Guide

Navigating through the "ZADAR Travel Guide 2024" is simple and efficient, designed to enhance your Zadar trip planning and on-ground experiences. Here's a brief guide on how to effectively utilize this resource:

1. Sections Overview: Familiarize yourself with the different sections of the guide, covering topics ranging from travel planning and accommodations to dining, transportation, and practical information.

2. Detailed Insights: Dive into each section to gain in-depth knowledge about Zadar's attractions, historical landmarks, hidden gems, local cuisine, transportation options, currency, language basics, safety tips, and more.

3. Maps and Recommendations: Use the maps provided in the guide to locate attractions, hotels, restaurants, and transportation hubs. Benefit from

recommended itineraries, must-visit spots, and off-the-beaten-path locations for a well-rounded Zadar experience.

4. FAQs and Resources: The Frequently Asked Questions (FAQs) section provides quick answers to common queries about Zadar. Explore the resources and contact information for valuable websites, tourist centers, emergency contacts, and apps to enhance your trip planning and safety.

5. Personalization: Use the insights and recommendations in this guide to tailor your Zadar itinerary based on your interests, budget, and travel preferences. Discover Zadar's unique charm at your own pace, whether you're a history buff, nature lover, food enthusiast, or adventure seeker.

By leveraging the insights, recommendations, and practical tips presented in this guide, you'll embark on a memorable journey in Zadar filled with discovery, cultural immersion, and unforgettable experiences. Enjoy every moment as you uncover the treasures of this captivating Croatian city.

Getting Started

Embarking on a trip to Zadar is an exciting adventure filled with historical wonders, natural beauty, and cultural experiences. Proper planning and preparation are essential to ensure a smooth and enjoyable trip. The "Getting Started" section of the "ZADAR Travel Guide 2024" provides valuable insights and tips to kickstart your Zadar exploration.

Travel Planning Tips

1. Research and Itinerary: Research Zadar's top attractions, events, and local culture. Create a flexible itinerary with must-visit landmarks like the Sea Organ, St. Donatus Church, and nearby national parks such as Paklenica or Krka.

2. Accommodation Booking: Secure your accommodation well in advance, especially during peak tourist seasons. Zadar offers a range of options, from luxury hotels in the city center to cozy guesthouses and budget-friendly hostels for backpackers.

3. Transportation: Plan your transportation to Zadar, considering options such as flights to Zadar Airport, bus and train connections, or driving if you're exploring Croatia's scenic routes. Research local transportation within Zadar, including buses, ferries, and rental cars, for convenient exploration.

4. Pack Essentials: Pack according to Zadar's climate and activities. Essentials include comfortable walking shoes for exploring cobblestone streets, swimwear for beach visits, sun protection, a reusable water bottle, and a camera to capture memorable moments.

Best Time to Visit Zadar

Understanding the optimal time to visit Zadar enhances your overall experience and allows you to enjoy its attractions to the fullest:

1. Summer (June-August): Peak tourist season with warm weather, ideal for beach activities, outdoor dining, and festivals like the Zadar Outdoor Festival and The Garden Festival. Expect crowded attractions and higher accommodation rates.

2. Spring (April-May) and Fall (September-October): Mild temperatures, fewer crowds, and pleasant weather for sightseeing, hiking in national parks, and exploring without the summer rush. Accommodation prices may be more reasonable during these shoulder seasons.

3. Winter (November-March): This is the off-peak season with cooler temperatures and occasional rainfall. It is ideal for budget travelers seeking

quieter experiences, exploring historical sites without crowds, and enjoying local cuisine in cozy restaurants.

Entry Requirements and Visa Information

1. EU/EEA Citizens: Citizens of the European Union (EU) and European Economic Area (EEA) countries can enter Croatia with a valid ID card or passport for stays up to 90 days within 180 days.

2. Non-EU/EEA Citizens: Visitors from non-EU/EEA countries may require a visa depending on their nationality. Check Croatia's official government websites or contact Croatian embassies/consulates in your country for specific visa requirements and application processes.

3. Schengen Zone: Croatia still needs to be part of the Schengen Zone. However, Schengen visa holders can enter Croatia without a separate

Croatian visa for short stays as per Schengen visa rules.

4. COVID-19 Travel Updates: Stay updated on travel advisories, entry requirements, and health protocols related to COVID-19. Check official government websites and airline guidelines for the latest information on testing, vaccination requirements, and quarantine regulations.

By incorporating these travel planning tips, understanding the best time to visit Zadar, and staying informed about entry requirements and visa information, you can embark on a well-prepared and memorable journey to this enchanting Croatian city. Enjoy the beauty of Zadar's historical landmarks, stunning coastline, and vibrant culture as you create unforgettable travel experiences.

Accommodations in Zadar

Suitable accommodation is crucial for a comfortable and enjoyable stay in Zadar. Whether you prefer luxurious hotels, budget-friendly options, or unique Airbnb rentals, Zadar offers various accommodations to suit every traveler's needs and preferences.

Choosing the Right Accommodation

1. Location: Consider the location based on your itinerary and preferences. Stay in the historic Old Town area for easy access to attractions, restaurants, and nightlife. Beachfront accommodations offer stunning views and beach access, perfect for sun-seekers.

2. Amenities: Determine your preferred amenities, such as free Wi-Fi, parking, air conditioning, swimming pool, spa facilities, or on-site dining options. Different accommodations offer varying amenities, so prioritize based on your requirements.

3. Budget: Set a budget range for accommodation expenses. Zadar provides options from luxury hotels with premium services to budget-friendly hostels and guesthouses ideal for cost-conscious travelers.

4. Reviews and Ratings: Research online reviews and ratings from previous guests on TripAdvisor, Booking.com, or Airbnb. Pay attention to comments regarding cleanliness, staff hospitality, location convenience, and overall guest experiences.

Top Hotels in Zadar

1. Falkensteiner Hotel & Spa Iadera: A luxurious 5-star beachfront hotel offering upscale rooms, a spa center, multiple dining options, and panoramic sea views. It is ideal for a relaxing and indulgent stay.

2. Boutique Hostel Forum: Located in the heart of Old Town, this stylish boutique hostel offers modern dormitories and private rooms with shared facilities. Perfect for budget travelers seeking a central location and social atmosphere.

3. Falkensteiner Family Hotel Diadora: This family-friendly resort offers spacious rooms, kids' clubs, water sports activities, pools, and entertainment options. It is ideal for families looking for a fun and comfortable stay.

4. Bastion Heritage Hotel—Relais & Châteaux: This historic boutique hotel is within the city walls. It offers elegant rooms, gourmet dining

experiences, and personalized service, perfect for a romantic getaway or luxury stay.

Budget-Friendly Options

1. Hostel Kolovare: A budget-friendly hostel near Kolovare Beach offering dormitory beds and private rooms with basic amenities. It is ideal for backpackers and budget travelers looking for a beachside stay.

2. Guesthouse Villa Maggie: Located in a quiet residential area, this family-run guesthouse offers affordable rooms with private bathrooms, free parking, and a cozy atmosphere. Great for travelers seeking a peaceful retreat.

3. Apartments Zadar Sunset: Airbnb and vacation rental options like Apartments Zadar Sunset provide comfortable and affordable accommodations with kitchen facilities, allowing

guests to save on dining expenses and enjoy a home-like experience.

Airbnb and Vacation Rentals

1. Flexibility: Airbnb and vacation rentals offer flexibility regarding room types, locations, and amenities. Choose from entire apartments, private rooms, or unique properties like villas and cottages based on your preferences.

2. Local Experience: Staying in Airbnb accommodations allows you to experience Zadar like a local, with hosts often providing insider tips, personalized recommendations, and cultural insights for a more immersive stay.

3. Cost-Effective: For families, groups, or long-term stays, Airbnb rentals can be more cost-effective compared to hotels, especially with options for self-catering and laundry facilities.

4. Safety and Regulations: Ensure you book through reputable platforms, read reviews, and communicate with hosts to clarify concerns or questions. Familiarize yourself with local regulations and safety measures for vacation rentals in Zadar.

By considering factors such as location, amenities, budget, and guest reviews, you can choose the right accommodation option in Zadar, whether it's a luxurious hotel, a budget-friendly hostel, or a unique Airbnb rental. This will ensure a comfortable and memorable stay in this captivating Croatian city.

Transportation in Zadar

Navigating transportation in Zadar is essential for a seamless and enjoyable travel experience. Whether arriving from another city in Croatia or exploring within Zadar, understanding how to access different transportation options is key to maximizing your time and exploring the city's attractions.

Getting to Zadar

By Air:

Zadar International Airport (ZAD) is the region's main gateway for air travelers. Several airlines operate flights to and from European cities, making it convenient for international visitors.

From the airport, you can reach the city center using various transportation modes:

- Airport Shuttle: Shuttle buses operate between the airport and Zadar city center, offering a direct and affordable transportation option. Check the schedule and ticket prices in advance.

- Taxi or Ride-Sharing Services: Taxi and ride-sharing services are available at the airport, providing a convenient door-to-door transportation option. Ensure you use official taxi services or reputable ride-sharing apps.

By Bus or Train:

Zadar is well-connected to major cities in Croatia and neighboring countries through an extensive bus and train network. Key transportation hubs include the Zadar Bus Station (Autobusni kolodvor

Zadar) and Zadar Train Station (Željeznički kolodvor Zadar). Consider the following options:

- Bus Services: Numerous bus companies operate routes to and from Zadar, offering comfortable and affordable travel options. Check schedules, book tickets online or at the station, and arrive early during peak seasons.

- Train Services: While train travel is less common for long-distance routes in Croatia, trains connect Zadar with cities like Zagreb and Split. Check Croatian Railways (HŽPP) schedules and ticket availability for train travel options.

Getting Around the City

Public Transport:

Zadar features a reliable and efficient public transportation system for exploring the city and nearby areas. The main modes of public transport include buses and ferries:

- City Buses: Zadar has a network of bus routes covering the city and suburbs. Tickets can be purchased from kiosks, newsstands, or the bus driver. Consider buying daily or multiple-ride tickets for cost savings.

- Ferries: Ferries connect Zadar with nearby islands like Ugljan, Pašman, and Dugi Otok, offering scenic and enjoyable day trips. Check ferry schedules and routes at the Zadar Ferry Port (Luka Zadar) or online platforms.

Walking and Cycling:

Zadar's compact city center and pedestrian-friendly streets make walking enjoyable. You can explore historic sites, waterfront promenades, and local markets. Consider renting bicycles for extended explorations or cycling along coastal paths for panoramic views.

Taxi and Ride-Sharing:

Taxis are readily available in Zadar and can be hailed on the street or booked through taxi companies. Ride-sharing services like Uber may also operate in the city, providing additional transportation options, especially during late hours or for specific destinations.

Renting a Car vs. Using Public Transport

Renting a Car:

Renting a car in Zadar offers flexibility and convenience, especially for exploring nearby attractions, rural areas, and national parks. Consider the following when renting a car:

- International Driving Permit: To drive in Croatia, you must have a valid driver's license and, if required, an International Driving Permit (IDP).

- Parking: Familiarize yourself with parking regulations, available parking lots, and fees in Zadar. Hotels may offer parking facilities or guide nearby parking options.

- Driving Tips: Follow local traffic laws, speed limits, and road signs. Be mindful of narrow streets and pedestrian zones in the Old Town area.

Public Transport Benefits:

Using public transport in Zadar offers cost-effective and eco-friendly travel options, especially within the city center and to famous tourist spots. Consider these benefits:

- Affordability: Public buses and ferries are budget-friendly, with options for single-ride tickets, day passes, and tourist cards offering discounts on transportation and attractions.

- Environmental Impact: Opting for public transport reduces carbon emissions and supports sustainable travel practices, preserving Zadar's natural beauty.

By understanding how to access transportation options to and within Zadar, including airport transfers, public transport routes, walking/cycling opportunities, and considerations for renting a car versus using public transport, you can plan your travels efficiently and enjoy a seamless experience exploring this captivating Croatian city. Adjust your choice based on your itinerary, budget, and travel preferences for a memorable visit to Zadar.

Exploring Zadar

Exploring Zadar is like delving into a living museum where ancient history blends seamlessly with modern innovations. From its rich historical sites to captivating modern installations, the city offers various attractions for travelers to discover and enjoy.

Historical Overview

Zadar's history traces back thousands of years, with influences from the Romans, Venetians, and Byzantines shaping its cultural and architectural heritage. The city's strategic coastal location contributed to its importance as a trading center and a hub of artistic and intellectual exchange in the region.

Top Attractions in Zadar

Old Town District

The Old Town of Zadar is a treasure trove of historical landmarks, narrow cobblestone streets, and charming squares. Key highlights include:

- Roman Forum: Dating back to the 1st century AD, the Roman Forum showcases ancient ruins, columns, and remnants of temples, providing a glimpse into Zadar's Roman past.

- Church of St. Donatus: A symbol of Zadar's early medieval architecture, this circular church from the 9th century is a must-visit for history and architecture enthusiasts.

Sea Organ and Greeting to the Sun

Two unique contemporary installations grace Zadar's waterfront:

- Sea Organ: Designed by architect Nikola Bašić, the Sea Organ harnesses the power of waves to create melodic sounds, offering a mesmerizing experience for visitors along the promenade.

- Greeting to the Sun (Pozdrav Suncu): Adjacent to the Sea Organ, this solar-powered installation features a circle of photovoltaic cells that light up in vibrant colors at sunset, symbolizing the harmony between nature and technology.

St. Donatus Church

Named after St. Donatus of Zadar, this cylindrical pre-Romanesque church is an iconic symbol of Zadar's architectural heritage. Climb to the top for panoramic city views and the nearby coastline.

Five Wells Square

Located near the Land Gate (Kopnena vrata), Five Wells Square (Trg pet bunara) is a historic gathering place surrounded by Renaissance-era architecture. The five wells were a vital water source during medieval times and added to the square's charm.

Archaeological Museum

Immerse yourself in Zadar's archaeological treasures at the Archaeological Museum, showcasing artifacts from prehistoric times to the Middle Ages. Highlights include Roman glassware, ceramics, and exhibits on ancient settlements in the region.

Hidden Gems and Off-the-Beaten-Path Locations

Exploring beyond the main attractions reveals Zadar's hidden gems and lesser-known spots:

- Church of St. Simeon: This 12th-century church, dedicated to St. Simeon, is near the

Land Gate. Admire the stunning architecture and Byzantine influences.

- Queen Jelena Madijevka Park: Escape the city buzz and relax in this tranquil park, which offers green spaces, walking paths, and panoramic views of Zadar's rooftops and the Adriatic Sea.

- Kalelarga: Wander along Zadar's main street, Kalelarga, which is lined with shops, cafes, and historic buildings. Experience the local culture and enjoy a stroll in this vibrant thoroughfare.

- Maraschino Liqueur Tasting: At local bars and distilleries, you can sample Zadar's famous Maraschino liqueur made from Marasca cherries. You can also learn about its centuries-old production methods and savor its unique flavor.

Travelers can uncover the city's captivating past and vibrant present by exploring Zadar's historical landmarks, modern installations, and hidden gems. Whether you're fascinated by ancient architecture, innovative art installations, or scenic parks, Zadar offers many experiences that resonate with every visitor's interests and curiosity. Enjoy the journey of discovery in this enchanting Croatian city.

Dining and Nightlife in Zadar

Exploring Zadar's dining and nightlife scene is integral to experiencing the city's vibrant culture and culinary delights. From traditional Croatian dishes to international cuisines and lively entertainment venues, Zadar offers diverse options to suit every palate and mood.

Local Cuisine and Must-Try Dishes

1. Seafood Delicacies: Zadar excels in seafood dishes as a coastal city. Try fresh Adriatic fish grilled or baked, seafood risotto (frutti di mare), octopus salad (salata od hobotnice), and black cuttlefish risotto (crni rižot).

2. Peka: A traditional Croatian dish cooked under a bell-like dome, combining meat (usually lamb or veal) or seafood with vegetables and herbs, slow-cooked to tender perfection.

3. Pag Cheese: Produced on the nearby island of Pag, this sheep's milk cheese (Paški sir) is known for its unique flavor, which is derived from the island's aromatic herbs and salted pastures.

4. Maraschino Liqueur: Sample Zadar's famous Maraschino liqueur, made from Marasca cherries, at local bars or enjoy it as a digestif after meals.

Best Restaurants for Traditional and International Food

1. Konoba Skoblar: This charming tavern in the Old Town serves authentic Dalmatian cuisine, including grilled fish, peak dishes, and homemade pasta, in a cozy atmosphere.

2. Pet Bunara: Pet Bunara offers a blend of traditional Croatian dishes and international flavors in the Five Wells Square area. It also has outdoor seating overlooking historic landmarks.

3. Foša: Near the famous Land Gate, Foša delights diners with its seafood specialties, creative interpretations of local recipes, and stunning harbor views.

4. Bruschetta Food & Wine Bar: Ideal for food enthusiasts seeking a modern twist on Croatian cuisine, Bruschetta offers a range of small plates, innovative bruschetta combinations, and a curated wine selection.

Cafes, Bars, and Nightclubs in Zadar

1. Cafes:

· Caffe Bar Lovre: Enjoy coffee with a view at this rooftop cafe overlooking Zadar's rooftops and the Adriatic Sea.

· Cafe Brazil: A cozy spot for coffee enthusiasts, offering specialty coffees, teas, and homemade pastries in a relaxed setting.

2. Bars:

· The Garden Lounge & Bar: Known for its trendy ambiance, craft cocktails, and live music, this bar attracts locals and tourists for evening socializing.

· Hemingway Bar: Inspired by the famous writer, this bar offers a sophisticated setting, premium cocktails, and a selection of cigars for a luxurious nightlife experience.

3. Nightclubs:

· Ledana Lounge & Club: Located near the waterfront, Ledana is a popular nightclub with themed parties, DJ performances, and a lively dance floor.

· Opera Club: Known for its electronic music events, themed parties, and vibrant atmosphere, Opera Club is a hotspot for late-night revelry in Zadar.

Tips for Dining and Nightlife in Zadar

1. Reservations: For popular restaurants, especially during peak tourist seasons, consider making reservations in advance to secure a table.

2. Local Recommendations: Ask locals or hotel staff for dining recommendations, hidden gems, or insider tips for authentic culinary experiences.

3. Explore Local Markets: Visit Zadar's markets, such as the Green Market (Tržnica), to sample fresh produce, local cheeses, olive oils, and artisanal products.

4. Dress Code: While casual attire is acceptable in most cafes and restaurants, some upscale venues may have a smart casual or formal dress code, especially in the evening.

Whether you're savoring traditional Croatian dishes, exploring international flavors, enjoying a leisurely coffee in a charming cafe, or dancing the night away in vibrant nightclubs, Zadar's dining and nightlife scene offers a dynamic and memorable experience for travelers seeking culinary delights and evening entertainment. Enjoy the gastronomic journey and lively nightlife in this captivating Croatian city.

Shopping in Zadar

Exploring Zadar's shopping scene offers a delightful experience for travelers looking to bring home unique souvenirs, local products, and memorable gifts. From traditional crafts to modern boutiques, Zadar's shopping districts and markets cater to various tastes and preferences.

Popular Souvenirs and Local Products

1. Maraschino Liqueur: Zadar is renowned for its Maraschino liqueur, which is made from Marasca cherries. Purchase a bottle or two to take home as a flavorful reminder of your time in the city.

2. Pag Lace: Handcrafted lacework from the island of Pag, known for its intricate designs and centuries-old tradition. As unique gifts, look for

lace tablecloths, napkins, or delicate lace accessories.

3. Olive Oil and Products: Croatia's olive oil is highly regarded for its quality. Explore local shops for extra virgin olive oil bottles, olive-based skincare products, and olive wood crafts.

4. Salt from Nin: Visit the nearby town to purchase sea salt harvested using traditional methods. Infused salts with herbs or spices make excellent culinary gifts.

5. Croatian Wines: Discover a range of Croatian wines, including local varieties from the Dalmatian Coast. Look for Plavac Mali red or crisp Pošip white wines to enjoy or share with wine enthusiasts back home.

Best Shopping Districts and Markets

1. Kalelarga: Zadar's main street, Kalelarga, is lined with shops, boutiques, cafes, and galleries. Explore the pedestrian-friendly street for clothing, accessories, local crafts, and souvenirs.

2. Forum Shopping Mall: Located near the Roman Forum, this modern shopping mall offers a mix of international brands, local retailers, food courts, and entertainment options under one roof.

3. Green Market (Tržnica): Immerse yourself in local flavors and aromas at the Green Market, where vendors sell fresh fruits, vegetables, cheeses, meats, and spices. It's a great place to experience everyday life in Zadar and purchase ingredients for a picnic or culinary souvenirs.

4. Antique Shops in Old Town: Browse antique shops and vintage boutiques in Zadar's Old Town for unique finds such as traditional ceramics, historical artifacts, retro clothing, and collectibles.

5. Flea Market (Buvljak): On weekends near the Kolovare Beach area, the flea market offers a treasure trove of secondhand items, antiques, handmade crafts, and quirky finds. Bargain hunters will enjoy exploring the stalls for hidden gems.

Tips for Shopping in Zadar

1. Opening Hours: Most shops in Zadar operate from morning until early evening, with some larger stores and malls extending hours, especially during tourist seasons.

2. Payment Methods: Major credit cards are widely accepted in shops and malls, but it's advisable to carry cash for smaller purchases, street vendors, or markets.

3. Local Artisan Workshops: Seek out artisan workshops and galleries in Zadar to purchase

handmade ceramics, jewelry, paintings, and crafts directly from local artists.

4. Quality and Authenticity: When purchasing local products like olive oil, wines, or lace, look for quality certifications or shop at reputable stores to ensure authenticity and value.

5. Packaging and Customs: Consider packaging fragile items securely for travel and be aware of customs regulations regarding food products, alcohol, and souvenirs when returning home.

Exploring Zadar's shopping districts, markets, and artisanal shops allows you to discover the city's cultural heritage, support local artisans and businesses, and find unique treasures to cherish or share with loved ones. Enjoy the shopping experience as part of your memorable journey in Zadar, Croatia.

Entertainment in Zadar

Zadar offers a vibrant entertainment scene that caters to diverse interests. Its offerings range from cultural performances and live music to outdoor activities and family-friendly attractions. Whether you're seeking relaxation by the sea, immersive cultural experiences, or thrilling adventures, Zadar has something for everyone to enjoy.

Cultural Performances

1. Theater Performances: Check out performances at the Croatian National Theatre in Zadar (HNK Zadar), showcasing theatrical productions, including dramas, comedies, and musicals. Keep an eye on their schedule for upcoming shows and events.

2. Music Concerts: Attend live music concerts featuring local bands, classical performances, jazz nights, and international artists at venues like the Arsenal (Arsenal Zadar) or outdoor stages during summer festivals.

3. Traditional Dances and Folklore: Experience Croatian culture through traditional dance performances, folklore shows, and music festivals celebrating local traditions and heritage.

Outdoor Activities

1. Beach Relaxation: Zadar's coastline offers picturesque beaches such as Kolovare Beach, Borik Beach, and Punta Bajlo, where you can sunbathe, swim in the crystal-clear Adriatic Sea, and enjoy water sports like kayaking, paddleboarding, and jet skiing.

2. Sunset Watching: Witness stunning sunsets at waterfront spots like the Sea Organ and Greeting

to the Sun, where nature's beauty is complemented by artistic installations, creating a unique ambiance.

3. Sailing and Boat Tours: Explore the nearby islands, hidden coves, and coastal landscapes on sailing and boat tours, or charter a private boat for a customized sea adventure.

Family-Friendly Attractions

1. Zadar Seafront: Take a leisurely walk or bike ride along Zadar's seafront promenade, lined with playgrounds, cafes, ice cream parlors, and interactive art installations for family fun by the sea.

2. Croatian National Museum Zadar: The Croatian National Museum offers educational and interactive experiences, showcasing archaeological artifacts, historical exhibits, and cultural treasures from the region.

3. Fun Parks and Water Parks: Plan a day of excitement at nearby fun parks like Mirnovec Adventure Park or water parks such as Fun Park Biograd, offering thrilling rides, slides, and entertainment for all ages.

Nightlife and Dining

1. Cafes and Restaurants: Explore Zadar's culinary scene with waterfront dining options, cozy cafes, seafood restaurants, and local eateries serving authentic Croatian cuisine, fresh seafood, and international flavors.

2. Bars and Nightclubs: Experience Zadar's nightlife at bars with live music, cocktail lounges offering creative drinks, and nightclubs hosting DJ nights, themed parties, and dance floors buzzing with energy until the early hours.

3. Summer Festivals: During summer, Zadar comes alive with music festivals, cultural events,

open-air concerts, and outdoor performances in venues like the Roman Forum and city squares, attracting locals and tourists alike.

Tips for Entertainment in Zadar

1. Event Calendars: Check local event calendars, tourism websites, and social media pages for upcoming concerts, festivals, theater performances, and cultural events during your visit.

2. Booking in Advance: For popular attractions, concerts, or guided tours, consider booking tickets to secure your spot, especially during peak tourist seasons.

3. Local Recommendations: Ask hotel staff, locals, or tour guides for recommendations on hidden gems, lesser-known attractions, and off-the-beaten-path experiences to enhance your entertainment options in Zadar.

4. Safety and Enjoyment: While enjoying nightlife and outdoor activities, prioritize safety measures, follow local regulations, and respect the natural environment to ensure a memorable and responsible experience in Zadar.

By exploring Zadar's diverse entertainment offerings, cultural attractions, outdoor adventures, and culinary delights, travelers can create unforgettable experiences and immerse themselves in the vibrant atmosphere of this captivating Croatian city. Enjoy Zadar's blend of history, culture, nature, and modern entertainment, making your visit truly memorable.

Sustainability and Responsible Tourism

As tourism grows in Zadar, sustainable practices and responsible tourism play vital roles in preserving the city's natural beauty, cultural heritage, and community well-being. Embracing sustainable initiatives benefits the environment and enhances the overall travel experience for visitors, ensuring long-term enjoyment of Zadar's treasures.

Sustainable Practices

1. Waste Management: Participate in waste reduction efforts using reusable water bottles, bags, and containers during your stay. Dispose of

waste responsibly in designated recycling bins and follow local waste management guidelines.

2. Energy Conservation: Conserve energy in accommodations by turning off lights, air conditioning, and electronic devices when not in use. Choose eco-friendly accommodations that prioritize energy-efficient practices and renewable energy sources.

3. Water Conservation: Practice water conservation by taking shorter showers, reusing towels, and reporting leaks or water wastage in accommodations. Support businesses implementing water-saving measures and technologies.

4. Support Local Economy: Patronize local businesses, artisans, markets, and restaurants that promote locally sourced products, sustainable practices, and fair trade principles. Choose authentic souvenirs from local artisans to support traditional crafts and cultural heritage.

Responsible Tourism Initiatives

1. Respect Cultural Heritage: Respect Zadar's cultural sites, monuments, and traditions by following guidelines, avoiding vandalism, and learning about local customs and etiquette. Participate in guided tours led by knowledgeable guides who emphasize cultural preservation.

2. Wildlife Protection: Choose responsible wildlife excursions and avoid activities that exploit or harm wildlife. Support ethical wildlife sanctuaries, marine conservation efforts, and eco-friendly tours that promote animal welfare and conservation education.

3. Nature Conservation: Responsibly explore Zadar's natural attractions, such as national parks, beaches, and coastal areas. Follow designated trails, avoid littering, and refrain from damaging flora, fauna, or natural habitats.

4. Community Engagement: Engage with local communities respectfully, learn about their culture, traditions, and challenges, and support community-based initiatives, cultural events, and sustainable tourism projects that benefit residents.

Sustainable Transportation

1. Public Transport: Utilize public transportation such as buses, ferries, and bicycles to reduce carbon emissions, ease traffic congestion, and support sustainable mobility options within Zadar and surrounding areas.

2. Walking Tours: Explore Zadar's historic districts, parks, and waterfront areas on foot through guided walking tours or self-guided walks, promoting active travel, cultural immersion, and reduced environmental impact.

3. Car-Free Days: Support initiatives promoting car-free days, pedestrian zones, and sustainable

urban planning in Zadar's city center to create a more walkable, bike-friendly, and livable environment for residents and visitors.

Responsible for Dining and Shopping

1. Sustainable Dining: Choose restaurants and eateries offering locally sourced ingredients, seasonal menus, sustainable seafood options, and eco-friendly practices such as reducing food waste and supporting organic farming.

2. Ethical Souvenirs: Purchase souvenirs from sustainable, recycled, or upcycled products. Avoid products made from endangered species, protected flora, or unsustainable resources.

3. Reduce Plastic Use: When shopping or dining, opt for reusable shopping bags, containers, and utensils. Support businesses that minimize single-use plastics offer refilling stations for water bottles and promote plastic-free packaging.

Engaging in Sustainable Tourism

1. Education and Awareness: Educate yourself and fellow travelers about sustainable tourism practices, local environmental issues, and cultural sensitivities in Zadar. Encourage responsible behavior and advocate for sustainable tourism principles.

2. Feedback and Support: Provide positive feedback and support to businesses, accommodations, and tour operators implementing sustainable practices. Share your experiences and recommendations with others to promote responsible tourism in Zadar and beyond.

3. Partnerships and Collaboration: Encourage collaboration among stakeholders, including local communities, businesses, government agencies, and NGOs, to develop and implement sustainable tourism strategies, conservation initiatives, and community empowerment projects in Zadar.

By embracing sustainable practices, supporting responsible tourism initiatives, and engaging in eco-friendly activities, travelers can contribute positively to preserving Zadar's natural environment, cultural heritage, and local communities for future generations. We can foster a more sustainable and rewarding travel experience in Zadar while promoting environmental stewardship and artistic appreciation.

Sample Itineraries

Creating a well-rounded and enjoyable itinerary for exploring Zadar involves combining historical and cultural attractions, outdoor experiences, culinary delights, and leisure activities. Below are sample itineraries catering to different interests and durations of stay, ensuring travelers make the most of their time in this captivating Croatian city.

Sample Itinerary 1: Cultural Immersion (3 Days)

Day 1: Historic Old Town Exploration

- Morning: Visit the Roman Forum, St. Anastasia's Cathedral, and Church of St. Donatus to glimpse Zadar's ancient and medieval history.

- Afternoon: Explore Kalelarga Street for shopping, cafes, and local souvenirs. Have lunch at a traditional Dalmatian restaurant.

- Evening: Witness the enchanting Sea Organ and Greeting to the Sun installations at sunset. Enjoy dinner with seafood specialties at a waterfront restaurant.

Day 2: Art and Museums

- Morning: Visit the Archaeological Museum to discover prehistoric and medieval artifacts.

- Afternoon: Explore contemporary art at the Museum of Contemporary Art or visit art galleries in the Old Town.

- Evening: Attend a cultural performance or music concert at Croatian National Theatre Zadar (HNK Zadar).

Day 3: Nature and Relaxation

- Morning: Take a boat trip to nearby islands such as Ugljan or Pasman for scenic views, swimming, and beach relaxation.

- Afternoon: Return to Zadar and enjoy leisure at Kolovare Beach or Queen Jelena Madijevka Park.

- Evening: Dine at a beachfront restaurant or enjoy a sunset cruise along Zadar's coastline.

Sample Itinerary 2: Family Fun (5 Days)

Day 1: Arrival and Orientation

- Arrive in Zadar, check into family-friendly accommodation and explore nearby amenities.

Day 2: Historical Highlights

- Morning: Visit the Archaeological Museum for interactive exhibits suitable for children.

- Afternoon: Explore the Old Town, including the Roman Forum and St. Donatus Church.

- Evening: Enjoy dinner at a family-friendly restaurant in the city center.

Day 3: Outdoor Adventures

- Morning: Visit Borik Beach for family-friendly swimming and water sports activities.

- Afternoon: Take a family sailing or boat tour to nearby islands, enjoying coastal views and snorkeling opportunities.

- Evening: Have a relaxed dinner at a seaside restaurant.

Day 4: Nature and Wildlife

- Morning: Visit the Zadar Zoo for a family-friendly wildlife experience.

- Afternoon: Explore Paklenica National Park for hiking trails suitable for families and picnic spots.

- Evening: Return to Zadar for dinner and evening strolls along the waterfront.

Day 5: Leisure and Departure

- Morning: Relax at Kolovare Beach or visit Fun Park Biograd for amusement rides and entertainment.

- Afternoon: Pack souvenirs and enjoy a farewell lunch at a local restaurant.

- Departure from Zadar with fond family memories.

Sample Itinerary 3: Food and Wine Experience (2 Days)

Day 1: Culinary Exploration

- Morning: Visit the Green Market (Tržnica) for fresh produce, local cheeses, and olive oil.

- Afternoon: Take a guided food tour of Zadar, sampling traditional dishes, seafood specialties, and Maraschino liqueur.

- Evening: Dinner at a gourmet restaurant featuring Croatian wines and Mediterranean cuisine.

Day 2: Wine Tasting and Cooking Class

- Morning: Join a wine-tasting tour to nearby wineries in the Zadar region, sampling Plavac Mali and Pošip wines.

- Afternoon: Participate in a cooking class focused on Dalmatian cuisine, learning to prepare seafood dishes or peak.

- Evening: Enjoy a farewell dinner with dishes prepared during the cooking class, paired with local wines.

These sample itineraries offer a balanced mix of cultural exploration, outdoor activities, family-friendly attractions, culinary experiences, and relaxation, showcasing the diverse offerings of Zadar for different types of travelers and interests. Customize your itinerary based on preferences, travel duration, and seasonal events to make your Zadar experience memorable and fulfilling.

Practical Information

Planning a trip to Zadar involves considering essential practical information to ensure a smooth and enjoyable travel experience. From understanding currency and language basics to prioritizing safety and emergency preparedness, being well-informed enhances your time in this beautiful Croatian city.

Currency and Banking

Currency:

Croatia's official currency is the Croatian Kuna (HRK). When traveling to Zadar, it is advisable to exchange currency at authorized exchange offices or banks or use ATMs to withdraw local currency. Major credit cards such as Visa and MasterCard are widely accepted in hotels, restaurants, and larger stores, but it is recommended to carry cash for smaller establishments and markets.

Banking Services:

Zadar has several banks and ATMs throughout the city, especially in the city center and near popular tourist areas. Banks typically operate on weekdays with limited hours on Saturdays. ATMs are accessible 24/7 and provide convenience for withdrawing cash in the local currency.

Language Basics

Official Language:

The official language spoken in Zadar and Croatia is Croatian. While English is widely understood, especially in tourist areas, learning a few basic Croatian phrases can enhance interactions and show respect for the local culture. Here are some useful phrases:

- Hello: Bok (informal) / Dobar dan (formal)

- Thank you. Hvala

- Yes: Da / No: Ne

- Excuse me: Oprostite

- Goodbye: Doviđenja

Safety Tips and Emergency Contacts

Safety Tips:

Zadar is generally a safe city for travelers, but it's essential to practice common sense safety precautions:

1. Stay Alert: Be aware of your surroundings, especially in crowded areas and tourist spots. Keep

valuables secure and avoid publicly displaying large amounts of cash or expensive items.

2. Use Reliable Transportation: Opt for licensed taxis, reputable ride-sharing services, or public transportation for safe travels within the city and to nearby areas.

3. Respect Local Laws and Customs: Familiarize yourself with local laws, cultural norms, and dress codes, especially when visiting religious sites or participating in cultural events.

4. Stay Informed: Monitor local news, weather updates, and any travel advisories during your stay. Follow guidance from local authorities in case of emergencies or unexpected situations.

Emergency Contacts:

In case of emergencies, dial the following numbers for assistance:

- Police: 192

- Fire Department: 193

- Medical Emergency: 194

- Roadside Assistance: 1987

Medical Services:

Zadar has hospitals, clinics, and pharmacies offering medical services. Ensure you have adequate travel insurance covering medical expenses and emergencies during your stay. Carry necessary medications and prescriptions in labeled containers.

Additional Tips:

1. Electricity: The standard voltage in Zadar is 230V, with a frequency of 50Hz. Type C and Type F plugs are commonly used, so bring appropriate adapters if needed.

2. Internet and Communication: Stay connected with local SIM cards or utilize Wi-Fi in accommodations, cafes, and public areas. International roaming may incur additional charges, so check with your mobile provider.

3. Transportation: Familiarize yourself with transportation options such as buses, ferries, and rental cars for exploring Zadar and nearby attractions. Plan routes in advance for convenience and time-saving.

4. Tourist Information Centers: Visit local tourist information centers for maps, brochures, guided tour bookings, and recommendations on attractions, events, and activities in Zadar.

By being prepared with practical information on currency and banking services, understanding language basics, prioritizing safety measures, and knowing emergency contacts, you can navigate Zadar confidently and enjoy a memorable and hassle-free travel experience in this charming Croatian city.

Frequently Asked Questions (FAQs)

As you plan your trip to Zadar, Croatia, you may have several questions regarding attractions, visas, transportation, dining, safety, and nearby excursions. Here are comprehensive answers to frequently asked questions to help you prepare for an unforgettable experience in Zadar.

1. What are the must-visit attractions in Zadar?

Zadar boasts a rich tapestry of historical landmarks, cultural sites, and natural wonders. Must-visit attractions include:

- The Roman Forum: Explore ancient ruins and historical artifacts dating back to Roman times.

- Sea Organ and Greeting to the Sun: Experience unique art installations on Zadar's waterfront that harness the power of nature and technology.

- St. Donatus Church: Admire the stunning architecture of this medieval church, a symbol of Zadar's heritage.

- Five Wells Square: Discover historic wells and Renaissance architecture in this charming square.

- Archaeological Museum: Dive into Croatia's archaeological treasures, including Roman artifacts and medieval exhibits.

2. What is the best time of year to visit Zadar?

The best time to visit Zadar depends on your preferences and interests:

- Summer (June to August): Ideal for beachgoers, outdoor activities, and vibrant festivals like the Zadar Outdoor Festival and Musical Evenings in St. Donatus.

- Spring (April to May) and Autumn (September to October): Mild weather and fewer crowds make these months perfect for sightseeing, hiking, and exploring without the peak tourist rush.

- Winter (November to March): There is a quiet atmosphere and festive markets during Christmas and New Year, suitable for travelers seeking a more relaxed experience and cultural immersion.

3. Do I need a visa to visit Croatia as a tourist?

For most tourists, Croatia allows visa-free entry for short stays (up to 90 days) within 180 days for nationals of many countries, including the European Union, the United States, Canada, Australia, and more. However, specific visa requirements vary based on your nationality and intended length of stay. Check with Croatian embassies or official government websites for up-to-date visa information.

4. How do I get from the airport to the city center?

Zadar Airport (ZAD) is approximately 8 kilometers from the city center. Travel options include:

- Airport Shuttle: Regular shuttle buses operate between the airport and the city center, offering convenient transportation for travelers.

- Taxi: Taxi are available outside the airport terminal for direct transfers to your accommodation in Zadar.

- Car Rental: Renting a car at the airport provides flexibility for exploring Zadar and nearby attractions at your own pace.

5. What are some local dishes I should try in Zadar?

Zadar offers a delectable array of traditional Croatian cuisine and seafood specialties:

- Black Cuttlefish Risotto (Crni Rižot): A savory dish with cuttlefish ink, rice, garlic, onions, and seafood flavors.

- Peka: Slow-cooked meat (lamb or veal) and vegetables baked under a bell-like dome infused with aromatic herbs and olive oil.

- Pag Cheese (Paški Sir): Sample this famous sheep's milk cheese from the nearby island of Pag, known for its unique flavor from salted pastures.

- Maraschino Liqueur: Sip on Zadar's iconic cherry liqueur, made from Marasca cherries, dates back centuries.

6. Is it safe to drink tap water in Zadar?

Yes, tap water in Zadar is generally safe for drinking and meets high-quality standards. Locals and tourists commonly drink tap water without issues. However, if you prefer, bottled water is widely available in stores and restaurants throughout the city.

7. What day trips can I take from Zadar?

Zadar serves as a perfect base for exploring nearby attractions and picturesque landscapes:

- Krka National Park: This renowned national park is approximately an hour's drive from

Zadar and offers stunning waterfalls, walking trails, and natural beauty.

- Plitvice Lakes National Park: Explore cascading waterfalls, turquoise lakes, and lush forests in this UNESCO World Heritage Site, about two hours from Zadar.

- Kornati Islands: Embark on boat tours to the Kornati archipelago, known for its pristine islands, crystal-clear waters, and excellent snorkeling opportunities.

These day trips offer enriching experiences for nature lovers, outdoor enthusiasts, and travelers seeking to immerse themselves in Croatia's stunning landscapes and biodiversity beyond Zadar's city limits.

By addressing these frequently asked questions, you can better plan and enjoy your visit to Zadar, Croatia, ensuring a memorable and fulfilling travel experience filled with cultural discoveries, culinary delights, and natural wonders.

Additional Resources

Planning a trip to Zadar involves gathering useful information, accessing helpful resources, and utilizing tools to enhance your travel experience. Here are valuable additional resources to supplement your trip planning and ensure a smooth and enjoyable visit to this charming Croatian city.

1. Official Tourism Websites and Apps

Visit Zadar Official Website:

The official tourism website for Zadar provides comprehensive information on attractions, events, accommodations, dining options, transportation, and practical travel tips. It offers detailed guides, maps, and suggested itineraries to help you plan your trip effectively.

Mobile Apps:

Download official tourism apps such as "Zadar Travel Guide" or "Zadar Offline Map & Guide" for offline access to maps, attractions, local tips, and navigation assistance while exploring the city.

2. Accommodation Booking Platforms

Booking.com, Airbnb, and Expedia:

These popular platforms offer accommodations, including hotels, guesthouses, apartments, and villas in Zadar. Filter options based on your preferences, budget, and location preferences to find the perfect place to stay.

Local Accommodation Websites:

Explore local accommodation websites and agencies specializing in Zadar and Croatian destinations for unique stays, personalized service, and insider recommendations.

3. Transportation and Travel Guides

Zadar Airport Website:

You can access flight information, airport facilities, transportation options, and car rental services directly from Zadar Airport's official website for seamless arrivals and departures.

Public Transport Apps:

Use apps like "Zadar Public Transport" or "Moovit" for real-time bus schedules, routes, ticket information, and navigation assistance within Zadar and surrounding areas.

4. Local Events and Activities

Event Calendars:

Check online event calendars, cultural websites, and social media pages for Zadar to stay updated on festivals, concerts, exhibitions, and special events during your visit.

Tour Operators and Guides:

Connect with reputable tour operators, guides, and excursion companies offering guided tours, outdoor activities, boat trips, and day excursions to nearby attractions from Zadar.

5. Travel Forums and Online Communities

TripAdvisor Forums:

Engage with fellow travelers, ask questions, read reviews, and gather insights from TripAdvisor forums dedicated to Zadar and Croatia for firsthand experiences and recommendations.

Reddit Travel Communities:

Join Reddit travel communities such as r/Croatia or r/Travel for discussions, travel tips, itinerary suggestions, and local insights shared by experienced travelers and residents.

6. Language and Cultural Resources

Language Apps:

Use language learning apps like Duolingo, Babbel, or Rosetta Stone to pick up basic Croatian phrases, improve communication skills, and enhance cultural interactions during your trip.

Cultural Guides and Books:

Explore travel guides, cultural books, and historical resources about Croatia, Dalmatia, and Zadar's heritage to deepen your understanding of the region's history, traditions, and local customs.

7. Safety and Emergency Contacts

Embassy Contacts:

Note the contact information for your country's embassy or consulate in Croatia for assistance with emergencies, lost documents, medical needs, or legal issues during your stay.

Local Emergency Numbers:

Save emergency contact numbers such as police, fire department, medical services, and roadside assistance in Zadar for quick access in case of emergencies.

Conclusion

Utilizing these additional resources and tools enhances your trip planning process, provides valuable insights, and ensures a rewarding travel experience in Zadar. Whether you're seeking accommodation options, transportation guidance, local events, language assistance, cultural insights, or emergency support, leveraging these resources empowers you to navigate Zadar confidently and make the most of your time exploring this captivating Croatian city. Safe travels, and enjoy your adventure in Zadar!

Conclusion

Exploring the enchanting city of Zadar unveils a tapestry of historical treasures, cultural richness, culinary delights, and natural beauty nestled along Croatia's stunning coastline. After delving into various aspects of planning, experiencing, and enjoying Zadar, it's time to reflect on the journey and the memories created.

Embracing Diversity and History

Zadar's allure lies in its rich history spanning Roman, medieval, and modern eras, evident in architectural marvels like the Roman Forum, St. Donatus Church, and Venetian-influenced structures. Exploring the Old Town's cobblestone streets reveals layers of heritage, museums, and hidden gems waiting to be discovered.

Enchanting Natural Landscapes

From sun-kissed beaches like Kolovare and Borik to nearby national parks such as Krka and Plitvice Lakes, Zadar offers a harmonious blend of coastal beauty and pristine nature. Sunset vistas at the Sea Organ and Greeting to the Sun create magical moments, highlighting Zadar's innovative art installations and natural wonders.

Culinary Delights and Local Flavors

Indulging in Zadar's gastronomic scene is a journey of savory delights, from seafood feasts with black cuttlefish risotto to savoring local cheeses like Pag cheese and sipping Maraschino liqueur. Exploring markets, cafes, and traditional konobas reveals the heart and soul of Dalmatian cuisine and hospitality.

Cultural Immersion and Experiences

Immersing in Zadar's cultural tapestry involves attending theater performances, exploring museums like the Archaeological Museum, and joining local festivals celebrating music, art, and traditions. Engaging with locals, learning basic Croatian phrases, and participating in hands-on activities like cooking classes deepen cultural connections.

Responsible Travel and Sustainability

As responsible travelers, embracing sustainable practices in waste management, energy conservation, and supporting local communities enriches the travel experience while preserving Zadar's natural beauty and cultural heritage for future generations.

Planning and Resources for Memorable Adventures

Utilizing comprehensive resources such as official tourism websites, accommodation platforms, and local apps and engaging with travel communities ensures seamless trip planning, access to valuable information, and immersive experiences tailored to your preferences.

Memories That Last a Lifetime

Whether strolling along the Riva promenade, admiring the intricate Pag lace, or embarking on day trips to nearby islands and national parks, each moment in Zadar leaves indelible memories of adventure, discovery, and cultural enrichment.

Embrace Zadar's Charms

In conclusion, Zadar captivates travelers with its blend of history, nature, culture, and hospitality, offering a mosaic of experiences that resonate long after the journey ends. Whether you seek relaxation by the Adriatic Sea, cultural insights in ancient streets, or culinary delights in local taverns, Zadar welcomes you to uncover its timeless allure and create cherished memories in Croatia's hidden gem along the Dalmatian coast. Plan your visit, immerse yourself in Zadar's wonders, and embark on a journey of discovery and delight in this captivating city by the sea. Safe travels and unforgettable adventures await in Zadar!

Made in the USA
Monee, IL
13 June 2024

59840044R00052